GW00715596

# THE LIFE & TIMES OF
# WILLIAM SHAKESPEARE

ACKNOWLEDGEMENT: I have been indebted throughout this little book to Samuel Schoenbaum's *William Shakespeare: A Compact Documentary Life* (Oxford, 1977), which I warmly recommend to anyone who wishes to learn more about the life.

# THE LIFE & TIMES OF

# **William Shakespeare**

BY
James Brown

This edition printed for, Shooting Star Press Inc, 230
Fifth Avenue, Suite 1212, New York, NY 10001

Shooting Star Press books are available at special discount
for bulk purchases for sales promotions, premiums, fund-
raising or educational use. Special editions or book
excerpts can also be created to specification. For details
contact – Special Sales Director, Shooting Star Press Inc.,
230 Fifth Avenue, Suite 1212, New York, NY 10001

This edition first published by Parragon Books
Produced by Magpie Books Ltd, 7 Kensington Church
Court, London W8 4SP
Copyright © Parragon Book Service Ltd 1994
Cover picture & illustrations courtesy of: Mary Evans
Picture Library; Christies Images.

This book is sold subject to the condition that it shall not,
by way of trade or otherwise, be lent, resold, hired out or
otherwise circulated without the publisher's prior consent
in any form of binding or cover than that in which it is
published and without similar condition being imposed on
the subsequent purchaser.
ISBN 1 57335 052 4
A copy of the British Library Cataloguing in Publication
Data is available from the British Library.

Typeset by Hewer Text Composition Services, Edinburgh
Printed in Singapore by Printlink International Co.

# STRATFORD

Shakespeare won fame and fortune in London. But he invested his money and kept his family in Stratford-upon-Avon. Some writers on the new London theatre scene of the late sixteenth century abandoned their home towns when they moved to the capital – Christopher Marlowe, for example, maintained no connection with Canterbury once he had left. But Shakespeare never cut himself off from his birthplace. It is tempting to read particular meaning into such loyalty, but it was quite common at the time for people to work for a while in London without ever completely settling in there. Local loyalties ran deep. There was little of the faceless anonymity of modern urban life – save, perhaps, in London. In a town the size of Stratford, at any rate, most people probably knew each other. One's relations with one's neighbours needed to be maintained if life was to go on smoothly. In Shakespeare's day, Stratford was a corporation, i.e. it governed itself. Every year a bailiff and fourteen aldermen, along with the fourteen burgesses they appointed, would handle the town's affairs, dealing with everything from breaking up fights to petitioning the Crown for assistance in the wake of a ruinous fire. In many ways, this was a community whose members were known to each other in a way which a modern city-dweller might well find intrusive, but which could also make for a close-knit sense of belonging.

Shakespeare was baptised on 26 April 1564. Tradition insists that he was born on 23 April 1564, partly so that the birthday of the National Poet should coincide with the Saint's Day of the National Saint, and partly for the sake of symmetry, in that he was to die on 23 April. However, one cannot be sure. He was born into an uncertain world. Of his seven siblings, three died in child-hood. He was lucky to survive childhood himself. The parish records laconically note in the list of burials for 11 July 1564, 'Hic incipit pestis': the dreaded plague had visited Stratford. Before it left, it would carry off some 200 souls. Infants and the infirm were in particular danger. Roger Green, a neighbour of the Shakespeares, had buried four children by the end of the year.

John Shakespeare had moved to Stratford by 1552; in that year, he was fined for leaving an unauthorized dung-heap in Henley Street. Originally he had come from Snitterfield, a village a few miles to the north. He was the son of Richard Shakespeare, a farmer, who died in 1561. He had left his disreputable brother Henry behind in Snitterfield, and taken to the trade of glover and whittawer (one who prepares white leather). He seems also to have traded in wool. For a time, everything went well. The Stratford records chart his early success in the purchase of property around Stratford, and the offices he held in the corporation.

By September 1558, when his first child was

born, he had married Mary, the daughter of Robert Arden, a modestly well-to-do farmer. Like John, she came from a village a few miles to the north of Stratford. William Shakespeare's career would take him to the city to work in a distinctively urban leisure-industry, but his roots, like those of the majority of the English people, were rural.

For a while, life was sweet. The Shakespeares were reasonably well off as middling people, and they were blessed with children, whose arrival one can chart through the entries in the baptismal register of Holy Trinity Church: Joan, 1558; Margaret, 1562; William, 1564; Gilbert, 1566; Joan (again – the first had died), 1569; Anne, 1571; Richard, 1574; and Edmund, 1580. John's business did well through the 1560s and into the 1570s. He was rewarded by his rise through the tiers of Stratford government to become Alderman in 1565. This meant that he would be addressed as Master Shakespeare, and on formal occasions he would have worn his gown of office. In the autumn of 1567, John was elevated to the highest office in the corporation when he became Bailiff. Again his position would have been visible to his fellow Stratfordians. He would have processed to the Guild Hall, and would have occupied a place of honour in church and, perhaps, when touring theatre companies came to perform. Even after his year in office, his standing was high: in 1571, when his neighbour Adrian Quiney was Bailiff, he was elected Chief Alderman and deputy. At some point while his fortune held, John Shakespeare applied to the College of Heralds for a Coat of Arms. This would have established his status as a gentleman, and passed it on to his heirs – an important matter in a society so conscious of rank.

The College got as far as drawing up a design for him, but the grant was never completed. The reason can be gleaned from the Stratford records. From 1576, his attendance at council meetings fell off. His colleagues were as indulgent to him as they could be, but finally, on 6 September 1586, they had to replace him because 'Mr Shaxspere doth not come to the halls when they do warn, nor hath not done of long time'. He had fallen on hard times. In 1578 he mortgaged part of his wife's inheritance. There were other transactions clearly designed to raise ready money. He seems to have had other, perhaps related, problems: in 1582 he undertook a legal process designed to restrain four fellow citizens from attacking him. Attendance at church was required by law, but in 1592 the Stratford authorities listed nine absentees whom they suspected kept away from church for fear of being arrested for debt. The hapless John Shakespeare was among them.

The precise cause of John Shakespeare's problems is not known. But times were hard in the late sixteenth century. The assumption behind the managed economy of Elizabethan England was that life went on much the same from one generation to the next. Their ideal was not the modern one of progress, but rather of stasis. Historical reality was very different – as John Shakespeare found out the hard way, and as his son discovered to his profit when he recouped the family fortunes in the newly-established professional theatre.

# FAITH AND LEARNING

There's no way of knowing with what
feelings Shakespeare regarded his father's
decline. It coincided with his early teens,
so he must have known what was going on,
and probably he could remember his father's
earlier high standing. Possibly the slight the
family suffered fuelled his ambition. Or his
father's plight may have furnished imagina-
tive stimulus by showing him the gulf
between social reality and the social ideal –
a theme of, for example, the cycle of history

plays that runs from *Richard II* through *Henry IV* to *Henry V*.

The instability of the age was more than economic. It was profoundly ideological. In 1534 Henry VIII had finally renounced the authority of the Pope: henceforth, the king would be the final arbiter of religion in England. Doctrinally he was a Catholic – what he needed was a divorce so as to secure a male heir. But the early sixteenth century also saw the advent of Protestantism under the leadership of such as Luther and Calvin. For the rest of the sixteenth century, religion in England would be a bone of political and bloody contention. Edward VI, who succeeded in 1547, was influenced by strongly Protestant relations. His half-sister Mary tried to force England back under Roman authority in her brief reign (1552–8). The methods by which she tried to save the souls of heretics earned her the sobriquet 'Bloody'. Elizabeth sought a workable compromise in Protestant doctrine in association with a liturgy that leaned towards Rome. It was a compromise which nevertheless cost a couple of hundred recusant 'Papists' their lives.

Many people conformed to successive edicts about what constituted the true faith – some just for the sake of a quiet life, and some, perhaps, because they were genuinely convinced that those set in authority over them genuinely had the right to settle such issues. Even so, it was disturbing to many. The authorities ended up making mutually conflicting and confusing claims about the allegedly eternal verities that underpinned (among other things) their own right to rule. In the process, time-honoured prac-

Title page from Shakespeare's works

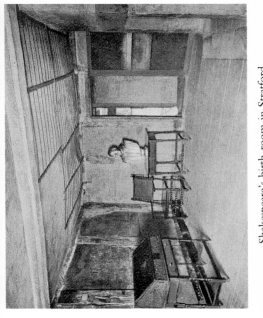

Shakespeare's birth-room in Stratford

tices could suddenly be declared illegal, and this was a society that liked to lean heavily on the sanction of tradition. It was bound to be unsettling. In Stratford, for example, in 1563 the appearance of the Guild Chapel was altered when the council mutilated its frescos, and then whitewashed them. In 1571 the council decided to replace the stained glass with plain. In both operations, John Shakespeare would have participated. Likewise, the traditional Mystery Plays – huge dramatic cycles dating back to the Middle Ages, portraying all human history from the Fall to the Last Judgement – finally fell prey to Protestant austerity, though the Coventry cycle continued just long enough for it to have been possible for the young William Shakespeare to have seen them.

Many had to hide their real beliefs. It is

possible that Shakespeare was among them. Late in the seventeenth century, a rumour was circulating that he 'died a Papist'. In the following century, when building work was being done in the former Shakespeare home in Henley Street, a document purporting to be John Shakespeare's Spiritual Last Will and Testament turned up in the rafters. If authentic, it would have proved that he was a Catholic. The great Shakespearean scholar, Edmund Malone, at first accepted it, but later claimed to have turned up evidence which discredited it. He promised to produce it in his planned life of Shakespeare. Unfortunately he never got around to writing it, and both documents have since been lost. The matter cannot be settled — and, of course, even if John Shakespeare was Catholic, it doesn't necessarily follow that his son was too.

One respect in which father and son were very different was their education. Shakespeare senior merely made his mark on official documents rather than sign his name. This does not necessarily mean that he was illiterate, but the schooling available in rural Snitterfield can't have amounted to much. It is true that William Shakespeare never went to university and that in later years Ben Jonson (a fellow dramatist and a man of formidable, largely self-taught learning) disparaged his 'small Latin and less Greek'. The notion that Shakespeare lacked formal education developed in the critical commonplace that Shakespeare was an untutored genius, untrammelled by formal learning. His work, accordingly, was not so much the product of skill as of mysterious intuition. As Alexander Pope put it, 'The Poetry of Shakespeare was inspiration indeed; he is not so much an Imitator, as an Instrument, of Nature; and 'tis not so just to say that he speaks from her, as that she speaks through him.'

One does not have to study Shakespeare for long to see the problem with this. Shakespeare's is certainly an uncommon talent, but it is backed by a range of sources and allusions which give the lie to the idea that Shakespeare was an undereducated genius. Merely by attending church, he would have become familiar with much of the Bible and the liturgy. But he also had some classical learning. He had a particular fondness for Ovid's *Metamorphoses*, and would later feel confident enough to beg comparison with the university-educated Marlowe in writing a long Ovidian poem, *Venus and Adonis*.

The odds are that he was educated at the King's New School in Stratford. Records do not survive, but it would have been natural; and, in any case, since his father was an alderman, it would also have been free. He would have gone to the petty school when he was about five, and then gone on to the grammar school itself. Hours were long, from about seven in the morning to five in the afternoon, with a couple of hours off around midday. The education reflected the intellectual upheavals of the Renaissance. Heavy emphasis was placed on linguistic skill – and Shakespeare would certainly have learned Latin, and maybe some Greek. There was a good deal of rote learning, but also other exercises more useful to the potential playwright, such as writing speeches appropriate to famous historical figures in given situations. There was also likely to be some training in speaking in public. The dramatist who later had Romeo exclaim 'Love goes towards love as school-boys from their books, But love from love, towards school with heavy looks' perhaps did not cherish fond memories of his school – days, but his works show that his education served him well.

Shakespeare was lucky. Education had taken off in England in his century. Had he been born earlier, or in the depths of the country far from a grammar school, he might never have become a writer. But it was not the only part of his mental world: he was also in touch with a mass of folklore, and old customs. The old and the new met in him and his works reflect the extraordinary mixture of influences and material that he integrated in them.

# MARRIAGE

It is not known exactly when Shakespeare left school, or why. Indeed, the only thing that is known about him for certain between his baptism and 1592, by which time he was an established actor-playwright in London, is that he got married in 1582. Like his own birth and death and the birth of his own children, it was part of his Warwickshire, rather than his London, life.

Shakespeare was eighteen; his bride, Anne

Hathaway, was probably twenty-six. Friends of the bride's family secured them a special licence from the Bishop of Worcester to get married after just one calling of the banns rather than the normal three. They had to enter into a bond to insure the Bishop against there proving to be any irregularity in the marriage. This was at the end of November 1582. They had good reason for their haste. On 26 May the following year, their first child, Susanna, was baptised in Stratford. The twins, Hamnet and Judith, would follow to the font on 2 February 1585.

What Shakespeare was doing at this time, apart from rushing up the aisle with an already pregnant bride, is not known. Early in the eighteenth century, Nicholas Rowe reported that he quit school to help his father as times got harder. That is plausible, and

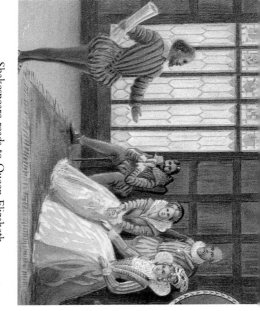

Shakespeare reads to Queen Elizabeth

THE LATE,
And much admired Play,
CALLED,
Pericles, Prince of
Tyre.

*With the true Relation of the whole Hi-*
*ſtory, adventures, and fortunes of*
*the ſaide Prince.*

Written by W. Shakespeare.

Printed for T. P. 1619.


THE
EXCELLENT
Hiſtory of the Mer-
chant of Venice.

*With the extreme cruelty of Shylocke*
the Iew towards the ſaide Merchant, in cut-
ting a iuſt pound of his fleſh. And the obtaining
of Portia, by the choyſe of
three Caskets.

Written by W. Shakespeare.

Printed by J. Roberts, 1600.


A
Moſt pleaſant and ex-
cellent conceited Comedy,
of Sir Iohn Falſtaffe, and the
merry VViues of VVindſor.

VVith the ſwaggering vaine of Ancient Piſtoll, and Corporall Nym.

Written by W. Shakespeare.

Printed for Arthur Iohnson. 1619.


A
YORKSHIRE
TRAGEDIE.

*Not ſo New, as Lamentable*
and True.

Written by W. Shakespeare.

Printed for T. P. 1619.

Title pages to four Shakespeare quartos

does put him in the right place to impregnate Anne, who lived in the village of Shottery, a walk over the fields west from Stratford.

Anne remains a deeply shadowy figure. All manner of strained deductions have sought to flesh her out. At twenty-six, she was getting a little old to be still unmarried, by the standards of the time. Was she, perhaps, out to trick a naïve teenager into marital shackles? Further confusion has resulted from the diocesan official managing to get her name completely wrong in the register recording the grant of the licence, where he turns her into 'Anne Whateley of Temple Grafton'. This has prompted some highly fanciful reconstructions of events. Perhaps Shakespeare really wanted to marry beautiful Anne Whateley, but the Hathaway clan were determined to see him do his duty

by their Anne. If one has a vivid imagina-
tion, one can picture the Hathaway friends
and Shakespeare racing each other to Worcester, each anxious to secure the necessary
marriage licence and beat the others to the
altar. Needless to say, no evidence supports
this. 'Whateley' is probably just a phantom
conjured by careless copying of notes.

In the absence of data, it is hard to evaluate
their marriage. Shakespeare spent a good
deal of time away from Stratford, while
Anne probably stayed behind. On the other
hand, he never really made his home in
London – he always seems to have regarded
Stratford as home, so it was perhaps natural
that he should keep his family there. The
super-gossip John Aubrey later reported that
he went back to Stratford each year. Relations with Anne may have been perfectly

amicable. There is, of course, his notorious will in which she gets nothing but the second-best bed, but that will be considered later.

# THE LOST YEARS

Somehow between 1582 and 1592 Shakespeare got himself from Stratford to London, from the likelihood of a career as a local business man, to dazzling success in the professional theatre. How?

At a literal level, the answer is easy: probably by foot. Whenever he first covered the hundred or so miles from Stratford to London he would have been poor, so he would have walked. It would have been a four-day journey.

But all the interesting questions remain. Did he go as soon as he was married? Or did he linger in Stratford, trying to save the family fortunes? Did he join the theatre immediately, or did he pursue some quite different career for a while? Much guesswork has gone into suggested answers to this last question. He has been pictured as a soldier, a sailor, a budding lawyer, a schoolmaster or a provincial player. As the great scholar Samuel Schoenbaum has wryly observed, the guessers like to model Shakespeare (as Man is said to model God) in their own images. So Shakespeare the lawyer is the idea of Edmund Malone, who had been a barrister; Shakespeare the sailor is the fruit of a commodore's idle hours; while Shakespeare the schoolmaster appeals to the professional pedagogue.

Did he set off with the intention of becoming an actor or a playwright, or did he merely set off at a venture, like Dick Whittington, vaguely hoping to make his fortune? One apocryphal tale pictures him fleeing Stratford for his life after poaching from the estate of Sir Thomas Lucy, and then making good in London. As with so much else, there's no way of knowing. However, it would not have been impossible for him to decide to work in the theatre. Theatre companies did occasionally stop in Stratford on tour. One such, the Queen's Men, ran into trouble in Thame in 1587, when one company member killed another in self-defence. They therefore arrived in Stratford a man short. Maybe Shakespeare filled the dead man's shoes. However, there were four other companies going through Stratford that year, and any of them might have inspired

William Shakespeare

Ophelia

Shakespeare to leave. Another team of scholarly sleuths have located him (under the name of Shakeshaft) with a private group of professional entertainers kept by the Houghton family in Lancashire. The case is ingenious, but unproven at best and at worst implausible.

However he got there, London was where he was to do the work that made his name.

# LONDON
# AND THE THEATRE

The city to which Shakespeare came was huge, lively, smelly, and unhealthy. With a population of perhaps a couple of hundred thousand, it was at least ten times bigger than Norwich or Bristol, its nearest rivals. But, though the population was vast in comparison with any other town in England, London was what is technically known as a demographic drain: in plain terms, people in London died faster than they were born.

Its huge population was sustained by immigration from all round the country.

London was uniquely vile, but also offered unique opportunities. Each hot summer the plague recurred. Fires were a major hazard in a city largely built of wood. Nor were there adequate public services to run such a city. The accepted model of local administration was suitable only on a much smaller scale – for example, in Stratford. Crime and public order were problems for which no one had an adequate solution. With no proper sanitation either, sewage flowed in open sewers to the Thames.

But London was also impressive. It was, after all, the centre of the royal court at one end of the town, and an unrivalled centre of commerce at the other, in the City. These two

authorities had different jurisdictions. Within the old city walls, the City fathers held
sway. The wealthy and the opportunistic and
the hopeful flocked to London, either to the
court, or to pursue lawsuits (Elizabethans
were notably litigious), or to attend Parlia-
ment. Such concentrations of people with a
little (or a lot of) spare cash naturally opened
the way for the enterprising to make money
entertaining them. There was bear- and bull-
baiting for those who had the stomach for it
– and on the whole the Elizabethans did.
There were brothels. And there were theatres.

The London theatre as a regular going
concern was an innovation. There had, of
course, been theatre in London on occasion
for a long time past – either in the great halls
of the Inns of Court or palaces, or on

makeshift stages in the yards of inns. But it was James Burbage, a master carpenter and sometime member of Leicester's Men (a theatre troupe), who spotted that there was enough business in London to justify a permanent, purpose-built theatre, which, straightforwardly enough, he called the Theatre. It had opened its doors in 1576 – just a decade or so before Shakespeare's arrival on the London theatre scene.

The Theatre was an outdoor theatre – that is to say, like the later Globe, it was a ring of galleries around a central yard open to the elements. In the yard there stood a stage. Its design may have owed something to the inn-yards in which companies had played.

The Theatre along with the Curtain, which was built the following year, were both in

Shoreditch, just to the north of the City. There was good reason for this. The City fathers were no friends to plays. They saw the assembly of an audience as a threat to public order and public health, and readily saw the plays themselves as immoral. Much literature had been explicitly moral. In a letter from the Lord Mayor and Aldermen to the Privy Council, plays are described as corrupting the young, as distracting apprentices and servants from their duty, and as a health risk. The City fathers express their opinion of plays:

'That neither in polity nor in religion they are to be suffered in a Christian commonwealth, specially being of that frame and matter as usually they are, containing nothing but profane fables, lascivious matters, cozening devices, and scurrilous behaviours, which are so set forth as that they move wholly to imitation and not to the avoiding of those faults and vices which they represent.'

Puritans were deeply troubled by the whole idea of play-acting. One preacher found that Burbage's Theatre was akin to 'the old heathenish theatre at Rome, a shew-place of all beastly and filthy matters'. Another called plays the 'plain devourers of maidenly virginity and chastity'. Such critics readily saw the pretence involved in drama as amounting to immoral deception. One's identity was conferred on one at birth by God Almighty and to act seemed to them to be meddling with God's work. This seemed to them to be particularly true of the boy-actors who played women's roles in the professional theatre. So Puritans readily saw plays as teaching one how 'to play the hypocrite, to cog, to lie and falsify', and all the other wickedness which a talent for dissimulation could pave the way to. Consequently, playhouses had to be located outside the City's jurisdiction – at first to the north, then from the 1580s on the south bank of the Thames. This was, of course, just the place where, for the same reason, the brothels were to be found.

Though the theatre's reputation with some was unsavoury and its neighbours disreputable, the theatre did have some powerful friends and some claim to a higher status than the City would have liked. In practice, the owners of the new playhouses and the acting companies that performed in them were business men. However, in theory, theatres existed for the sake of the court, and the players were the retainers of the nobility, and sometimes of royalty. Professional companies were kept in London to be ready to entertain the great when they were called upon. While they waited, they were permitted to rehearse. The public performances to which ordinary folk flocked were rehearsals for royal entertainment, so, as Queen Elizabeth put it when conferring legal protection on one company in 1574, they were 'as well for the recreation of our loving subjects, as for our [i.e. the Queen's] solace and pleasure . . .' The court was loath to have its entertainment wrecked by Puritans or City fathers or anyone else. It tended to resist the City's attempts to destroy the theatre.

The theatre was thus ambiguously and interestingly placed, socially, legally and geographically.

# AN UPSTART CROW

Such was the town and the business to which the young Shakespeare came – probably at some point in the mid to late 1580s. Since he was an actor as well as a writer, he most likely got work at first as one of the hired men of an acting company – one of the actors hired as employees by the senior actors, who had a stake in the company and were known as sharers. There's no way of knowing whether he had embarked on a career in the theatre with a view to becoming a playwright or

Ann Hathaway's cottage

Shakespeare jubilee in Stratford

not, but by the late eighties he must have
started to write plays. For the greater part of
his career he would enjoy a uniquely secure
relationship with one company, the Lord
Chamberlain's Men, later renamed the
King's on James I's accession in 1603. But
at first he must have worked as a writer on
the same insecure terms as most others.

A touring company of players does not need
many scripts. They can offer the same
handful of shows in every town they come
to. A settled company has to lure spectators
back time and again with new attractions.
The new profession of playwright swiftly
emerged to supply the need. One entrepre-
neur, Philip Henslowe, kept a diary of his
operation which records the continual turn-
over of scripts, rushed together by writers
working at speed and often in teams. Writing

plays was seldom well rewarded. The dramatist would sell his script outright to the company. Nor could he readily get more by publication. The actors discouraged it because, in the absence of copyright, it would make the play available to their rivals. So the writer would have to churn out more and more to make a living.

It is likely that Shakespeare at least started by writing with others, even though he would later tend to work alone. However, by 1592 he had built up a reputation great enough to attract the bile of a rival.

In 1592 Robert Greene lay on his death-bed. He had been to Cambridge, and taken his B.A. and M.A. degrees. He had then misspent his life. Having run through his wife's money, he financed his drinking and his mistresses out of the modest profits of professional writing, which ran to the creation of several plays. As he gasped his last, he (the authorship is open to question, but it probably was him) scribbled one last work: *Greene's Groatsworth of Wit, Bought with a Million of Repentance*. He addressed a special warning about the players to his fellow professionals:

'Yes, trust them not: for there is an upstart crow, beautified with our feathers, that with his *tiger's heart wrapped in a player's hide* supposes he is as well able to bombast out a blank verse as the best of you; and, being an absolute *Johannes Factotum*, is in his own conceit the only Shake-scene in a country.'

Greene reserves particular animosity for Shakespeare. He even alludes to one of his works. In *Henry VI, Part 3* as Queen Margaret taunts the defeated Duke of York he castigates her for having a 'tiger's heart wrapp'd in a woman's hide'. Clearly, by 1592 Shakespeare was established as a writer, and his lack of a university education clearly wasn't holding him back – much to Greene's annoyance.

The denouement of the incident also reveals something else about Shakespeare. Greene had expired entrusting his last thoughts to Henry Chettle to see them through the press. In the author's absence, Chettle had to take the flak for his dead friend. A few months later, Chettle offered his apologies to two writers who had taken offence. He dismisses one of them (possibly Christopher Marlowe) as a person with whom he has no wish to be closer acquainted. To the other, he is more

Shakespeare at work

Macbeth and the witches

conciliatory. He regrets, now that he has met the victim, that he did not cut the offending passages from the manuscript,

'. . . because myself have seen his demeanour no less civil than he excellent in the quality he professes: besides, divers of worship have reported, his uprightness of dealing, which argues his honesty, and his facetious [i.e. polished] grace in writing that approves his art.'

It is eloquent testimony to Shakespeare's amiability and respectability. Chettle is addressing the two issues on which Greene attacked him: his status and his art.

Shakespeare made his name at first with his plays about English history. The three parts of *Henry VI* and Richard III show how the Tudor dynasty emerged to put an end to a period of chaos and civil war. The plays add up to a work on a huge scale. Whether Shakespeare originally intended to spin his material out so far or not, the plays are bold and ambitious. As recent productions have shown, they are also robustly stageworthy: a great secular epic of nationhood. He also wrote a blood-curdling tragedy set in ancient Rome called *Titus Andronicus* (the only play for which a contemporary illustration of actors at work survives). Other early plays may have included *The Two Gentlemen of Verona* and *The Taming of the Shrew* – most recent scholarly estimates have put *The Comedy of Errors*, which used to be thought an early play, rather later in his output.

However, if Shakespeare thought that he had settled into theatre work for life, he was soon proved mistaken.

# PLAGUE AND POETRY

When the plague claimed more than thirty or so a week, public assemblies (except for church services) would be banned. In January 1593 the dreaded plague-orders were issued by the Privy Council:

'We think it fit that all manner of concourse and public meetings of the people at plays, bear-baitings, bowlings and other like assemblies for sports be forbidden . . .'

Save for short periods of respite, the theatres would not reopen until the winter of 1594. By then, perhaps 11,000 Londoners had perished.

Anyone who could, escaped to the country. London became a ghost town. Grass started to sprout in the streets. Those hapless wretches who could not or would not leave went in fear. One actor, who was playing on the continent in 1593, returned home to Shoreditch to find his entire family dead.

Theatre companies either went on tour or disbanded. It is possible that Shakespeare set off with one company, but that it fell apart after a short while. The sheer length of the period of closure would force virtually all the companies to re-form.

Various fanciful notions as to what Shakespeare did next have been advanced. But,
while it is hard to know exactly where he
was, there's no secret about what he was
doing, for at least part of the time. Baulked of
making a living in the theatre, he turned to
poetry. Marlowe had set a fashion for a kind
of Ovidian poem in English with *Hero and
Leander*. Shakespeare now outdid him with
*Venus and Adonis*. It appeared in 1593,
evidently printed from a carefully prepared
manuscript. Shakespeare had also got himself
a patron – a nobleman who would pay for
the honour of having a work dedicated to
himself. Shakespeare presented what he
called his 'unpolished lines' to Henry
Wriothesley, the young Earl of Southampton. The poem caters for a delicately bawdy,
modish, sophisticated taste. It also proved to
be a big seller. Sixteen editions had appeared

by 1640. Hardly a popular work today, then it was so avidly read and reread that many copies disintegrated.

In 1594 Shakespeare followed his poetic début with a graver poem, *The Rape of Lucrece*: the gruesome tale of the rape of a virtuous wife by a powerful king. Once again the work was dedicated to Southampton, possibly in terms rather warmer than last time, which may suggest that Shakespeare had come to know his patron a little. Though less successful than *Venus and Adonis*, it did well enough.

These works show Shakespeare trying (and succeeding) to break into a completely different market. He certainly can't have planned this two-year hiatus in his theatrical career, and once it was over he did not care

Titania and Bottom

The Globe Theatre

to go back to trying to make a career out of poetry. But he had proved himself extraordinarily adaptable. He did go on writing poetry – the Sonnets indicate as much. But he would never again try to reach the public primarily through the printing-press. Most other publications of his work during his lifetime were carelessly prepared for the press, and were often a response to pirated editions. Twenty of his plays were unpublished when he died.

A later writer, William Davenant, who put about the story that he was Shakespeare's bastard son, reported at the end of the seventeenth century that (as Nicholas Rowe relayed it) 'My Lord Southampton, at one time, gave him a thousand pounds, to enable him to go through with a purchase which he had heard he had a mind to'. The sum is implausibly huge – and Southampton in any case had money problems at the time. But it is possible that as Shakespeare's patron he came up with a lump sum. If so, then we can reasonably guess what Shakespeare used it for.

# THE LORD
# CHAMBERLAIN'S MEN

Queen Elizabeth spent the Christmas of 1594 in Greenwich. The leading theatre company of the day followed downstream, to entertain her. Later, the three leading members of the company went to get their fee. They were Richard Burbage, the son of the carpenter and impresario, James Burbage; William Kempe, the leading clown of his day, famed for his ability to improvise and to ride the audience; and William

Shakespeare. This was the company Shakespeare would stay with for the rest of his career. His appearance in the royal accounts almost certainly means that he had become a sharer in the company – if Southampton had proved a generous patron, Shakespeare may well have used his money to buy a stake in the Lord Chamberlain's Men.

The combination of the different roles of actor, playwright and sharer in the acting company was highly advantageous. Shakespeare would know the business inside out – he could count on being able to cast his plays as he chose, and could write with specific performers in mind. But better was to follow.

Like many blessings, this silver lining came wrapped up in a black cloud. The company's

London home was James Burbage's Theatre, which stood on land leased from Giles Allen. The lease was due to expire on 13 April 1597. Allen seemed loath to let the Theatre continue. James Burbage cast about for an alternative. His commercial instincts were as good as ever: he chose the old refectory of what had been Blackfriars monastery. It was in the district still known as Blackfriars, which was in the City, but, for historical and legal reasons, lay outside the City's jurisdiction. What he envisaged was an indoor theatre catering for a smaller, more upmarket audience. He spent £600 getting the place and converting it, only to have the local residents pull strings with the Privy Council and have the project scotched. In January, while he was still trying to negotiate the new lease, James Burbage died.

His heirs, Richard and his brother Cuthbert, were now in a mess. They were about to lose the Theatre and they had sunk their capital in an unusable replacement. April came and went. The company played on for a while, and then had to move to a temporary home, possibly the Curtain. Giles Allen planned to pull the Theatre down 'and to convert the wood and timber thereof to some better use'. But the Burbages got wind of his intentions. In a daring move in which Shakespeare very likely participated, they decided to steal their theatre back. On the night of 28 December 1598, with Allen out of the way in the country, the Burbages, along with Peter Street, their carpenter, and about a dozen others, dismantled the Theatre, and did a flit with it across the river to the south bank, where it was reborn as the Globe. Allen was predictably livid and sought to vent his wrath

Hamlet at the grave

Romeo and Juliet

on these 'riotous persons', as he called them, by suing them. But the Burbages had laid their plans carefully; Allen didn't have a leg to stand on.

The Burbages were short of capital, so in order to finance the new project they formed a syndicate, which included five members of the Lord Chamberlain's Men (not counting Richard Burbage himself). Among these five was Shakespeare. The deal was signed on 21 February 1599. The effect was to give the Lord Chamberlain's Men unprecedented power over their own affairs. No other acting company also held shares in the theatre-owning company. It was a unique arrangement. It also ensured that the leading actors kept a bigger proportion of their profits.

Financially, Shakespeare was clearly doing well. A year or two after joining the company, he revived his father's claim to a Coat of Arms from the College of Heralds, and carried it through to a successful conclusion. In 1597 he bought New Place, the second biggest house in Stratford. His investments in Stratford would continue over the next few years: 107 acres just north of the town and a cottage near New Place in May 1602; an interest in tithes on 'corn, grain, blade and hay' from Old Stratford in July 1605.

He had started to lay up wealth in Stratford. But all was not well. His only son, Hamnet, died there and was buried on 11 August 1596.

While in London, he seems to have lived near his work. Records of unpaid taxes suggest that he must have been living in Bishopsgate, just south of the Theatre, and that he probably moved south when the Lord Chamberlain's Men's base moved.

He would have been acting throughout this period – and not just in his own plays. He is listed among the actors who first played Ben Jonson's comedy *Every Man in His Humour*. He would have played some part in running the company. But the only part of his activity that we can still appreciate is his writing.

He had learned valuable lessons during his time away from the stage. He now commanded a greater range of tone than any other dramatist. His output showed astonishing variety – not just considered overall, but within individual plays. He could now put utterly different worlds on-stage in a single play: in *A Midsummer Night's Dream* we see the court, the lovers, the citizens rehearsing their play, and the fairies; in the two parts of *Henry IV* the action ranges panoramically over the king's austere court, Falstaff's *louche* Cheapside, the doomed rebels, and Justice Shallow's Gloucestershire. Even when the characters all share the same place, as in *Romeo and Juliet*, one senses in the quality of their language that different characters inhabit their own individual worlds – the Nurse's homely bawdy, Mercutio caught up in the intricacies of his own wit, Friar Lawrence full of well-meant, but ineffectual, proverbial wisdom, and Romeo and Juliet transported by their love into matchless powers of expression.

The Theatre at Stratford in the nineteenth century

Shakespeare's tomb at Stratford

# JACOBEAN SHAKESPEARE

The new century brought with it a change of monarch – at long last. Elizabeth had reigned for as long as some people could remember, and by the 1590s people had begun to anticipate her end, which contributed to the distinctive *fin de siècle* feel of the decade. For Shakespeare and the Lord Chamberlain's Men now installed at the Globe, the new century brought further confirmation of their position as the leading theatre group. When Elizabeth finally died on 24 March

1603, James VI of Scotland progressed south to assume the English crown as James I. On 17 May the patronage of the company changed, when a royal warrant styled them 'our servants'. They were now the King's Men. It was not just a name – they would perform at court more often than any other company.

Shakespeare was at the height of his powers, and starting to turn to darker themes, to dilemmas that resisted the resolutions the comedies of the nineties had often managed to achieve. Most of the great tragedies probably belong to the first decade of the century: *Hamlet* (possibly from the very end of the last century), *Macbeth*, *King Lear*, *Othello* and *Antony and Cleopatra*. He probably also wrote a group of notably disquieting comedies at about this time, such as

*Measure for Measure*, whose nominally happy ending is less than wholly convincing, and in some modern productions it has been completely subverted to leave the play's awkward questions about the proper balance between justice and mercy, and between punishment and desire, hanging unanswered at the end.

Victorian scholars used to like to relate the change in the tone of the work to alleged developments in Shakespeare's life. Could it be that Hamnet's untimely death had poisoned his view of life? Or should one blame his father's death in 1601? But it is impossible to relate life to work in this way. It was an age given to caustically satirical plays, tragic as well as comic, and to the asking of awkward questions. Such hints as we get of Shakespeare's off-stage life do not make it sound particularly black. He invested more money in Stratford. His professional standing was so high that printers tagged his name to other plays in order to make them sell. Many of the anecdotes about him (though not authoritative) continue to testify to his personal good humour. Aubrey speaks of his being 'very good company' and having 'a very ready and pleasant smooth wit'. There's one tale relating to Richard Burbage making an assignation with a lady citizen:

'Upon a time when Burbage played Richard III, there was a citizen grew so far in liking with him that before she went from the play she appointed him to come that night unto her by the name of Richard the Third. Shakespeare overhearing their conclusion went before, was entertained, and at his game ere Burbage came. Then message being brought that Richard the Third was at the door, Shakespeare caused return to be made that William the Conqueror was before Richard the Third.'

The story is probably apocryphal, but around 1604 Shakespeare found himself an onlooker in the midst of an even funnier and much more bizarre tale, which went on record when it later became the subject of a lawsuit in 1612 and Shakespeare had to testify. He had taken lodgings in the house of Christopher Mountjoy, a refugee Huguenot and maker of ladies' headgear. Also in the house were Christopher's wife and daughter, both called Mary, and his apprentices, among them Stephen Belott. In 1612 Belott was bringing the case, having married Mary Mountjoy the younger, without ever receiving what he thought they had agreed as a dowry. The whole situation was complicated by the Mountjoys independently consulting the astrologer Simon Forman: Mrs Mountjoy, about an affair she was having with a mercer; and Christopher Mountjoy, about business and the future of his apprentices. Forman's diary reveals that at one point Mrs Mountjoy hid in his house: it's tempting to envisage a farce in which both Mountjoys descend on Forman at once. One of the servants remembered that Mountjoy 'did send and persuade one Mr Shakespeare that lay in the house to persuade the plaintiff [Belott] to the same marriage'. Another witness recalled that Shakespeare was in the midst of the financial negotiations, which would have made his testimony crucial. But when it came to the point, neither he nor anyone else could remember the nitty-gritty.

This is the stuff of city comedy of just the kind that younger rivals such as Thomas Middleton were writing at the time. But Shakespeare chose never to use his real-life experiences.

Not everything was so pleasant or entertaining. His youngest brother, Edmund, had turned actor and fetched up in London. He never did particularly well, but in his brief life managed to father a bastard (buried at St Giles' Church without Cripplegate on 12 August 1607). Edmund himself was dead by the end of the year, buried at St Mary Overy (now Southwark Cathedral) on New Year's Eve. It was a fairly expensive funeral; it's hard to see who but William could have provided it.

But even if Shakespeare suffered his share of misfortune, his company and his personal fortunes were going from strength to strength. Finally, in 1608, they got their hands on the Blackfriars theatre that James Burbage had wanted to move to back in 1597. But instead of abandoning the Globe, they kept it on for summer performances. They formed a syndicate to run Blackfriars, and again Shakespeare was part of it. Artistic possibilities were multiplied by the new indoor theatre with its smaller capacity of maybe 700 as opposed, the Globe's 2,000-to 3,000.

In 1609 Thomas Thorpe published a collection of Shakespeare's sonnets. The overwhelming majority of them had never appeared in print before. They seem, at times, to be telling a story of an emotional triangle featuring a well-born young man, the poet, and a mysterious Dark Lady. But no one is sure whether the Sonnets are in the 'right' order, or even whether we have them all. They have a tantalizing air of barely concealed autobiography which has set scores of hopefuls off on the vain attempt to reconstruct Shakespeare's inner life by finding the real identities of the young man and the Dark Lady. Particular attention has been lavished on Thomas Thorpe's dedication of the sonnets:

TO.THE.ONLY.BEGETTER.OF.
THESE.ENSUING.SONNETS.
Mr. W.H.ALL.HAPPINESS.
AND.THAT.ETERNITY.
PROMISED.
BY.
OUR EVER-LIVING.POET.
WISHETH.
THE.WELL-WISHING.

WILLIAM SHAKESPEARE

ADVENTURER.IN.
SETTING.
FORTH.
T.T.

Who is 'Mr. W.H.', and what exactly is
Thorpe saying about his relationship to the
work? Is he the same as the young man of the
sonnets, or was he just someone who hap-
pened to end up with some of the manu-
scripts (quite possible given that poetry often
circulated in this form)? Could he be the Earl
of Southampton, Henry Wriothesley, with
his initials reversed? Or could he be William
Herbert, Earl of Pembroke? One ingenious
suggestion was that 'W.H.' stands for 'Will
Himself'. No one's ever been much the
wiser for these attempts, and Thorpe's ec-
centric punctuation only contributes to the
confusion. Is he, for example, promising

eternity to the 'well-wishing adventurer' or to 'Mr. W.H.'? As with the move towards allegedly darker themes in the plays, one cannot draw conclusions about Shakespeare's life from the evidence of his work. In his own mind, at any rate, one suspects that he kept his life on a perfectly ordinary plane back in Stratford.

# RETIREMENT

Towards the end of his writing life, he was spending more and more time back in Stratford. His mother had been buried on 9 September 1609. Her death may have caused Shakespeare to give more personal attention to his business interests there. In any case, he seems to have reduced his London commitments. In the Mountjoy case, he is described as being 'from Stratford', which may suggest that he no longer had regular London lodgings. By 1613 he had written his last solo works – most importantly, that final group of plays concerned with reconciliation, often achieved in an atmosphere of mystery or magic. Oddly enough, he did buy a house in Blackfriars in 1613, but that seems to have been as an investment rather than for his own use. There were to be no more plays.

He went back to live among the same families that he'd grown up with. He was a prominent, well-to-do gentleman. His brother Gilbert, who had followed a career in business, died early in 1612; Richard followed about a year later.

There are some records of his involvement in local affairs. In 1614 he put up a visiting preacher at New Place, and reclaimed 20d. from the corporation for the preacher's drink. He had a stroke of luck that summer when a huge fire swept through Stratford leaving his property intact. Shortly afterwards, he got involved on the periphery of a local controversy about plans to enclose common fields at Welcombe. Things came to a comical head when one lot of men turned out to dig a trench to establish the enclosure, shortly followed by their opponents who, after some deft legal footwork, filled it in again. Shakespeare seems to have kept his head down during this argument, and by the time the lawsuit that resulted had been straightened out, he was buried in Holy Trinity with most of the rest of John Shakespeare's family.

The tortuous provisions of his will suggest that his main concern was to see that the bulk of his property descended intact to his male heirs. The death of his only son, Hamnet, had already made this awkward. But he clearly hoped that one or other of his daughters would continue the line. Susan had married a successful physician, John Hall, on 5 June 1607. Their only child, Elizabeth, was born the following year. Shakespeare's other daughter, Judith, only married in 1616. It soon transpired that her husband, Thomas Quincy, had fathered a bastard – both baby and mother died in childbirth about a month after Thomas and Judith's wedding.

By then, Shakespeare knew he was dying. The provisions of his will, revised for the last time on 25 March, suggest scant faith in Thomas Quincy, who would be sentenced for his misdeeds the following day. He seems to have changed his mind as he wrote, and instead of leaving £150 to his son-in-law, left it to Judith instead, and even then with provisos. He makes a number of small bequests to local friends, and he remembers 'my fellows John Hemyngyes, Richard Burbage and Henry Cundell', colleagues in the King's Men, to whom he leaves money for rings as was the custom. His wife is very nearly omitted entirely. Finally, at a late stage, he leaves her 'my second-best bed with the furniture' (i.e. the trappings for the bed itself). It looks, at first sight, like a final vindictive swipe from beyond the grave. But it is impossible to be sure. The second-best bed may have been their own marriage bed. Anne's omission otherwise can be explained if one assumes that Shakespeare expected Anne's rights to be secure during her lifetime under common law. But there is no way to know.

Shakespeare's will is not rich in sentiment. It has a practical purpose to fulfil. The bulk of the property is to go to John and Susan Hall, with a view to its eventually descending to their male heirs. Failing that, it might go to Judith male heirs if she ever had any. Judith's three children were born after Shakespeare's death, and Susan might have had more children. Shakespeare was trying to lay claim to the future. In this he completely failed. He died on 23 April 1616, and his direct line was extinct by 1670.

Ironically, it was two of the colleagues to whom he had made uncomplicated bequests for rings who saved something for him. In 1623 they decided to honour their dead colleague by publishing a collected edition of his plays. This included twenty plays that had never been published before, and which would have been completely lost but for this. Shakespeare seems not to have been bothered about them. Presumably he regarded them as ephemeral. His friend and rival, Ben Jonson, had other ideas. He was far from idolizing Shakespeare, whom elsewhere he criticized for taking insufficient care, and then went on, carefully balancing praise and criticism:

'He was indeed honest, and of an open, and free nature; had an excellent phantasy, brave notions, and gentle expressions, wherein he flowed with that facility, that sometime it was necessary he should be stopped . . .'

However, he rose to the occasion in the poem to Shakespeare's memory that appeared in the Folio:

'Triumph, my Britain, thou hast one to show,

   To whom all Scenes of Europe homage owe.

He was not of an age, but for all time!'